All About
Dogs

American Pit Bull Terriers

Becky Noelle

AV2
www.av2books.com

AV2

Step 1
Go to www.av2books.com

Step 2
Enter this unique code

ZQCKXXSF7

Step 3
Explore your interactive eBook!

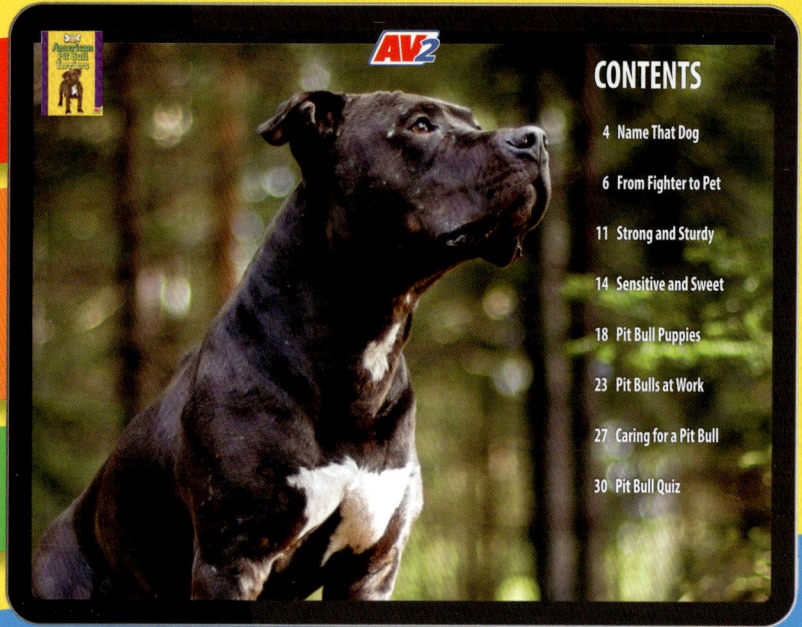

CONTENTS

AV2 is optimized for use on any device

Your interactive eBook comes with...

Contents
Browse a live contents page to easily navigate through resources

Audio
Listen to sections of the book read aloud

Videos
Watch informative video clips

Weblinks
Gain additional information for research

Try This!
Complete activities and hands-on experiments

Key Words
Study vocabulary, and complete a matching word activity

Quizzes
Test your knowledge

Slideshows
View images and captions

This title is part of our AV2 digital subscription

1-Year K–5 Subscription
ISBN 978-1-7911-3320-7

Access hundreds of AV2 titles with our digital subscription.
Sign up for a FREE trial at www.av2books.com/trial

All About Dogs

American Pit Bull Terriers

Contents

Name That Dog

Which dog has a strong, square jaw?

Which dog can be any color?

Which dog has a past as a fighter?

Which dog once helped to catch livestock?

There is only one answer...

The American pit bull terrier!

From Fighter to Pet

American pit bull terriers, often called pit bulls, originally came from Great Britain and Ireland. In the 19th century, bulldogs and terriers were bred together. The new breed became known as the pit bull.

Bulldogs are strong dogs that were used for **bullbaiting**. Terriers were bred as hunting dogs. **Breeders** wanted both the strength of a bulldog and the agility of a terrier to make stronger hunting and fighting dogs, and so the pit bull was born.

Great Britain and Ireland are islands off the northern coast of Europe. Scotland, Wales, and England are all part of Great Britain.

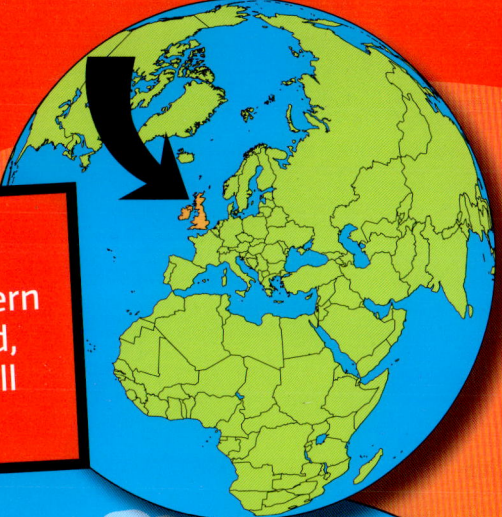

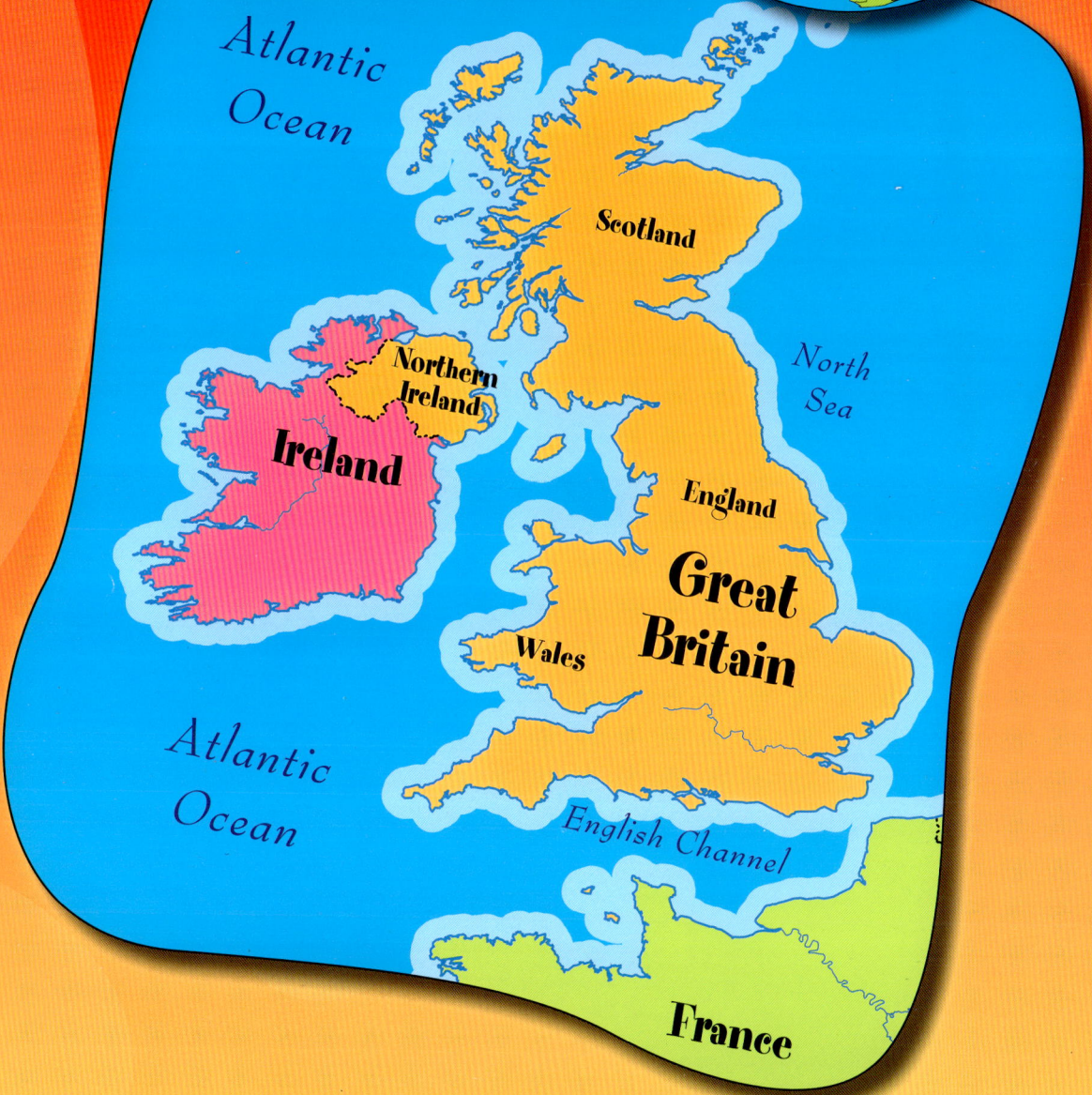

Atlantic Ocean

Scotland

Northern Ireland

Ireland

North Sea

England

Great Britain

Wales

Atlantic Ocean

English Channel

France

Pit bulls were brought to the United States in the late 19th century. People kept pit bulls both as family pets and as working animals.

American pit bull terriers are often grouped together with other "pit bull" dog breeds. American Staffordshire terriers, Staffordshire bull terriers, and American bully dogs are also included in this group. All four "pit bulls" have similar origins but are different breeds.

Not all dog breed registries recognize the American pit bull terrier as an official breed. The American Kennel Club (AKC) does not. However, the American pit bull terrier was recognized by the United Kennel Club (UKC) in 1898, and by the American Dog Breeders Association (ADBA) when it was founded in 1909.

Bullbaiting became illegal in Great Britain in 1835.

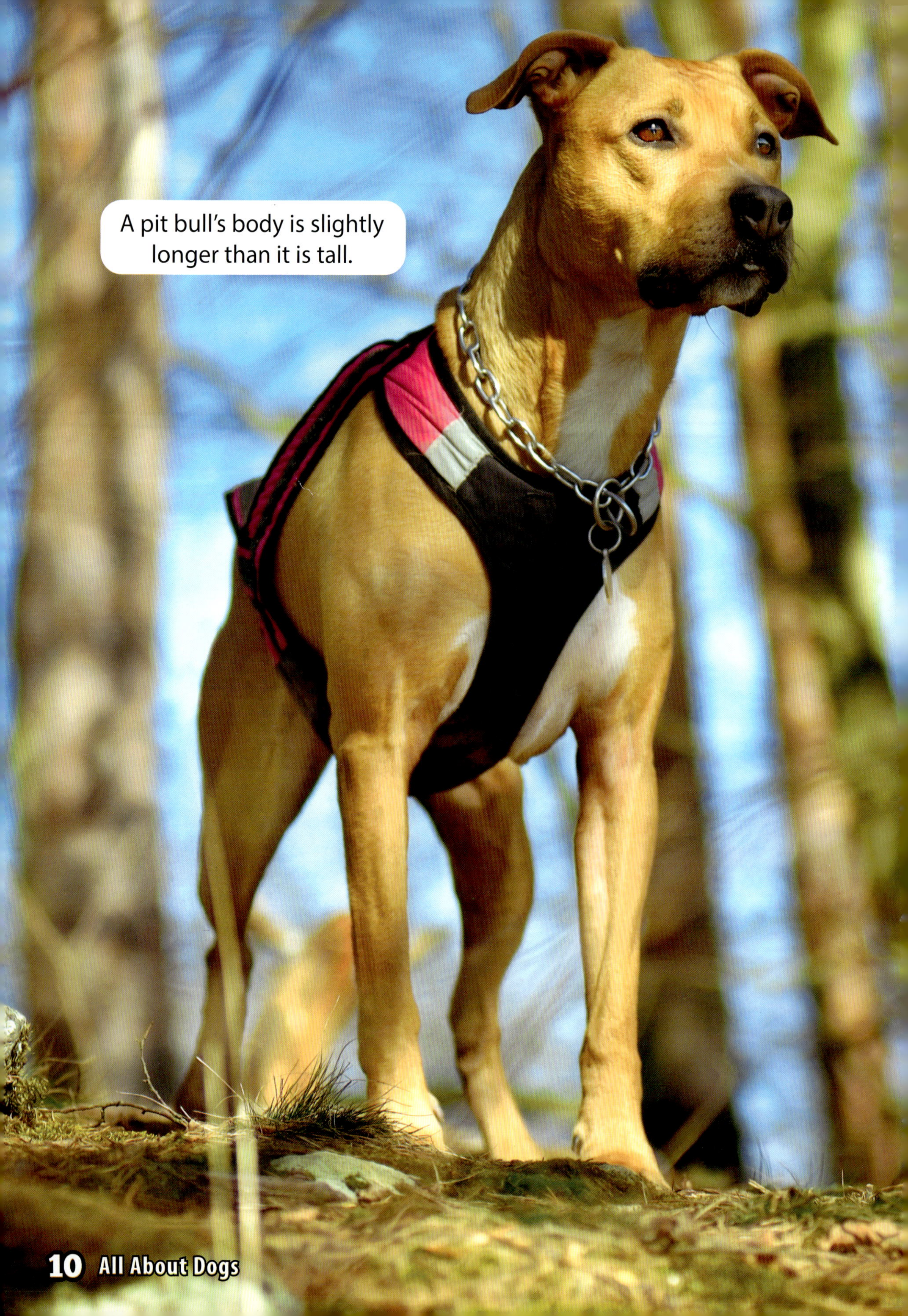

A pit bull's body is slightly longer than it is tall.

Strong and Sturdy

American pit bull terriers are medium-sized dogs. They are powerful animals with large, flat heads and strong, square jaws. Pit bulls also have a deep chest and a **sturdy** body.

Male pit bulls usually weigh between 35 and 60 pounds (16 and 27 kilograms). They are between 18 and 21 inches (46 and 53 centimeters) tall. Female pit bulls are smaller. They typically weigh between 30 and 50 pounds (14 and 23 kg) and are 17 to 20 inches (43 to 51 cm) tall.

Pit bulls have been used as "catch dogs," grabbing and holding farm animals with their strong jaws.

Docking and cropping are illegal in some countries, but are allowed in the United States.

American pit bull terriers come in all colors. However, they often have some white on their chest or face. Pit bulls have a short, shiny coat that is easy to **groom**.

A pit bull's ears are small and stand up a little bit. These ears may be cropped to make them stand up all the way. To crop a puppy's ears, a veterinarian cuts off part of each ear and tapes the ear to something hard for a few weeks.

Pit bulls have a somewhat short tail that is thicker at the base and ends in a point. Some dog owners have their pit bull's tail docked. Docking is cutting a dog's tail shorter when it is a very young puppy.

A pit bull's nose is large, with wide nostrils. It can be one of many colors, including red or black.

Sensitive and Sweet

Although many people think of pit bulls as **aggressive** dogs, owners typically find them quite happy and goofy. Pit bulls are very attached to their owners. Some people call them "wiggle butts" because of how excitedly they greet their families. Pit bulls will also lean up against their owners to show **affection**.

Pit bulls are very smart and **sensitive**. They are willing to listen and want to do what their owner asks. This makes them good learners.

Pit bulls do not make effective guard dogs. They are often very friendly toward strangers.

Pit bulls are known for being very good climbers. Owners should have tall, sturdy fences around their yards.

Pit bulls are good at many different physical activities, including jogging, hiking, swimming, and playing ball.

Pit bulls must be trained well from a very young age. They need clear and **consistent** rules so that they will be well-behaved dogs. A pit bull's owner has to earn his or her dog's respect to make sure it will listen.

Pit bulls can be very active dogs. Getting a large amount of exercise will help a pit bull burn off energy. This also helps make a pit bull learn to follow rules.

Sometimes, pit bulls can be aggressive toward other dogs. This is because one of the original uses for pit bulls was as fighting dogs. Owners may need to keep their pit bulls on leashes and away from other dogs. Proper training and **socialization** can also help a pit bull learn to behave around other dogs.

Pit Bull Puppies

It takes about nine weeks for pit bull puppies to be ready to be born. Pit bull puppies are born with their eyes and ears closed. Their eyes open after about two weeks.

A pit bull puppy grows quickly. After a pit bull puppy is four weeks old, it may be ready to eat solid puppy food. After about eight weeks, the puppy is ready to leave its mother and go to a new home. By the time it is a year old, a pit bull is considered an adult dog.

Pit bull litters typically have between 5 and 10 puppies.

All puppies need to learn how to control their bites. Owners can train puppies to play gently without hurting humans.

The first four months are very important for socializing a pit bull puppy. A pit bull puppy should meet many new people and dogs. People should hold and pet the puppy, touching its paws, ears, and mouth to help make it more comfortable with others. Owners should never be rough with or mean to a pit bull puppy. A scared puppy may grow to become an aggressive adult.

Pit bull puppies should have water whenever they need it. They do best with three small meals a day. Owners should help puppies get used to people being around while they eat. They can do this by hand-feeding the puppies.

Like other puppies, pit bulls start to grow their adult teeth when they are about three months old. While this is happening, they need plenty of toys to chew on.

Although Sergeant Stubby's breed has never been completely confirmed, he was likely at least part pit bull.

Pit Bulls at Work

In the past, pit bulls were working farm dogs. They were used to help catch **livestock** that had escaped. Pit bulls were also bred to fight other dogs. Breeders chose dogs that were aggressive toward other dogs but not toward humans. Dog fighting was popular in both the United States and Great Britain, but is illegal today.

Pit bulls have worked in the military, too. A pit bull mix named Sergeant Stubby was a hero in World War I. He served as a mascot for a group of soldiers and helped them know when there was danger. Stubby would also help find hurt soldiers on the battlefield.

Pit bulls are strong dogs. Some can pull weights of more than 5,000 pounds (2,268 kg).

Pit bulls have a good sense of smell. They can work as drug-sniffing dogs, helping police officers find illegal drugs. Pit bulls can also use their noses to help with search and rescue, finding missing people that need help.

As most pit bulls love people and are very friendly, they can be used as therapy dogs. Therapy dogs visit sick and elderly people that might need comfort. Some pit bulls can help children learn to read by acting as good listeners.

Pit bulls are strong and athletic. Many owners train pit bulls to compete in events. Pit bulls can learn to catch disks, dive off docks, or pull heavy weights.

Some people call pit bulls "nanny dogs" because they are often gentle around children.

Pit bulls may need sunscreen on their coats if the weather is hot and sunny.

Caring for a Pit Bull

Pit bulls require firm and consistent care. Owners will need to train a pit bull throughout its life. This is why pit bulls are best suited for experienced dog owners.

Pit bulls can be great family dogs if socialized properly. They should never be chained up or left alone outside for a long time. Pit bulls like to be close to their human family.

Pit bulls need regular physical activity. They should have a chance to exercise for at least an hour every day.

Owners should brush their pit bull's teeth every day.

Owners should trim their pit bull's nails about once every two weeks. Pit bulls have short fur, so they do not need to be brushed very often. Owners should be careful to use a gentle brush on their pit bull's coat.

Pit bulls can have sensitive skin. Having baths too often may make their skin itchy. Owners can help by using a shampoo made for sensitive skin. A pit bull should have its ears cleaned about once a month. If a pit bull is scratching its ears and shaking its head often, it may have an ear problem and should be brought to a veterinarian.

With the right training and socialization, pit bulls can be very fun and loving pets. A healthy pit bull will live between 12 and 14 years.

Pit bulls can be allergic to grass. Pit bull owners should call a veterinarian if they see any bald spots, bumps, or rashes on their dog's skin.

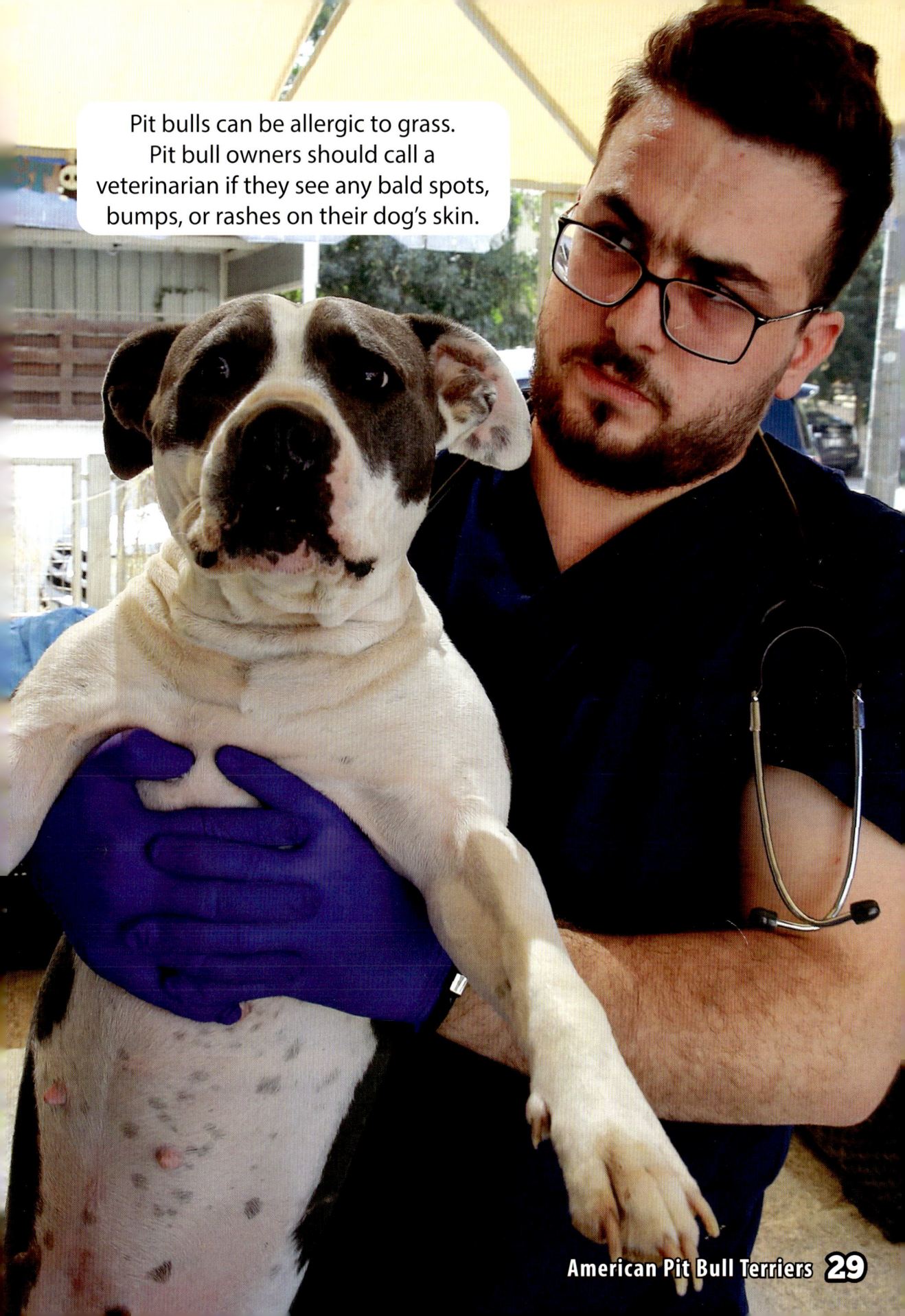

Pit Bull Quiz

Q: When was the American Dog Breeders Association (ADBA) founded?

A: 1909

Q: What are common pit bull nose colors?

A: Red and black

Q: When does a pit bull puppy need to be socialized?

A: During the first four months of its life

Q: What were pit bulls originally bred for?

A: Catching livestock and fighting

Q: How much weight can some pit bulls pull?

A: More than 5,000 pounds (2,268 kg)

Q: Where were pit bulls first bred?

A: Great Britain and Ireland

Key Words

affection (uh-FECK-shun): a feeling of liking someone or something

aggressive (uh-GRESS-iv): mean, unfriendly, or trying to start a fight

breeders (BREED-urz): people who mate animals for specific traits

bullbaiting (BUL-bay-ting): making a dog fight a bull

consistent (cun-SIH-stint): always done in the same way

groom (GROOM): to brush and clean the coat of an animal

livestock (LYV-stok): farm animals such as horses, cows, sheep, and goats

sensitive (SEN-sih-tiv): easily upset or hurt by something

socialization (so-shul-eye-ZAY-shun): learning how to act around other people and animals

sturdy (STUR-dee): strong and not easily broken

Index

AV2

Get the best of both worlds.

AV2 bridges the gap between print and digital.

The expandable resources toolbar enables quick access to content including **videos**, **audio**, **activities**, **weblinks**, **slideshows**, **quizzes**, and **key words**.

Animated videos make static images come alive.

Resource icons on each page help readers to further **explore key concepts**.

Published by AV2
276 5th Avenue
Suite 704 #917
New York, NY 10001
Website: www.av2books.com

Library of Congress Cataloging-in-Publication Data

Names: Noelle, Becky, author.
Title: American pit bull terriers / Becky Noelle.
Description: New York, NY : AV2, 2022. | Series: All about dogs | Includes
  index. | Audience: Ages 8-11 | Audience: Grades 2-3
Identifiers: LCCN 2021009595 (print) | LCCN 2021009596 (ebook) | ISBN
  9781791140496 (library binding) | ISBN 9781791140502 (paperback) | ISBN
  9781791140519
Subjects: LCSH: American pit bull terrier--Juvenile literature.
Classification: LCC SF429.A72 N64 2022 (print) | LCC SF429.A72 (ebook) |
  DDC 636.755/9--dc23
LC record available at https://lccn.loc.gov/2021009595
LC ebook record available at https://lccn.loc.gov/2021009596

Printed in Guangzhou, China
1 2 3 4 5 6 7 8 9 0   25 24 23 22 21

032021
101320

Project Coordinator: John Willis
Designer: Terry Paulhus

Photo Credits
Every reasonable effort has been made to trace ownership and to obtain permission to reprint copyright material. The publisher would be pleased to have any errors or omissions brought to its attention so that they may be corrected in subsequent printings. The publisher acknowledges Alamy, Getty Images, Newscom, and Shutterstock as its primary image suppliers for this title.